Hygge Ho

Cozy, Danish Ideas for House Interiors

By

Barry Gray

Hygge Home

Copyright © 2017

ISBN: 9781521154526

Warning and Disclaimer

Publisher Contact

Skinny Bottle Publishing

books@skinnybottle.com

Goals

I want you to do me a favor.

I want you to stop reading this book for a moment and think about your home. Perhaps even spend a few minutes walking through the various rooms. How do you feel about each room? Do they feel 'homely' or are they more practical? Or, alternatively, is there a sense of unorganized chaos?

Perhaps you are quite comfortable in your home? Or, maybe you feel that this sense of comfort is non-existent and that it is something you would like to achieve, and yet, that achievement may feel like the impossible dream?

Before I delve into the world of hygge and how it applies to your home, I want you to be honest with yourself and how you feel about not just each and every room, but even the outside of your home. After all, I'm about to take you on a journey through your house, moving from room to room, helping you to transform it into something that is indeed more comfortable, cozy, the kind of place that you want to come back to after a hard day at work.

Yes, this is entirely possible, and the best part is that it will require less work than you were perhaps expecting. In fact, often the most subtle of changes can have a profound effect on the energy or atmosphere that transcends each and every room.

But it is only possible if you can sit and be critical of yourself. Be critical of color schemes. Be honest about those items in your home that serve no real purpose apart from 'looking good' or 'filling a space.' Admit to yourself that you do indeed have clutter. That there are aspects of your home that are just not as harmonious as you would like them to be.

OK, I understand if you now feel as if this book is going to be negative, but I can assure you that this is not the case. However, change is not always easy. Actually, it is very rarely easy although that's not a reason to avoid it.

My aim here is not to get you to conduct a complete overhaul of your home from top to bottom. No, that's not what I am about. Instead, I am simply going to guide you towards making those changes that will not only refresh a room but give your entire home a better energy and feel to it. By the end, and if you implement the various changes that I will discuss, you will hopefully have that harmonious home you have always dreamt of.

So, what are we waiting for?

Dealing with the Formalities

Prior to offering you various tips regarding your home, I need to get a few formalities out of the way. I have a feeling that a healthy percentage of people will have read my introduction and thought, 'well that sounds nice, but how are you going to do that, Barry?'

Well, that's why I'm starting with these formalities and in particular a quick discussion on the concept that provides us with the framework for everything that is to follow. That concept is hygge, and it is something that can change your entire life if you are willing to just open your heart and mind so it can then work its own unique brand of magic.

This concept can cover virtually every facet of life. Its ability to change how you view your existence is undoubtedly rewarding thanks to the way in which it provides you with a more positive outlook and greater peace of both your mind as well as your soul.

But that's for elsewhere.

For now, all I want to say is that 'hygge' has no direct translation into English. Instead, the best I can do is say that it's more about a feeling and a sense of things that include peace, calmness, serenity, and that cozy feeling that I mentioned in the first few paragraphs.

It's something that the Danes have perfected. Let's face it, hygge is their concept so it makes sense that they would be the best at it. Indeed, such is its power that it is often attributed to the fact that the Danes are always in the mix when it comes to the happiest nation on the planet.

However, we are able to take so many aspects of this entire theory of hygge and apply it to your home. After all, it's something that the Danes have worked on over the years with other Scandinavian countries following suit.

Just think about the Scandinavian style within the world of interior design, and I'm not just meaning Ikea. It's all about light, space, clean lines; everything has its place and a role to play in the home. Practicality is enormous. It creates a sense of calm in each room, a spot in every room where you feel as if you can get lost in the moment no matter what it is that you are doing.

For some, this sounds idyllic, and to many it is. But then, why should your home not feel like this? Surely your home is supposed to be your own space, no matter its size, that you can just relax in? After all, shouldn't your home be your own special sanctuary? Should you not be able to see it as your place of refuge from the outside world? Surely you would then want this to be as comfortable as possible?

I think that I can perhaps best sum up the idea of hygge in the home by mentioning these few points.

- It should be snug and cozy.

- It should be peaceful and nurturing.

- Prepare to use cushions, blankets, and rugs like never before.

- Light will be used in different ways to create an atmosphere.

- Warmth will transcend your home.

- You will be free of clutter, and things will be organized.

- You are going to enjoy coming home rather than dreading it.

So, hygge is going to be our base for all that is to follow. However, we do have a considerable amount to cover, so we need to get things moving.

Dealing with the Feeling of Comfortable Living

To those that attempt to incorporate hygge into their home life, there is a need to focus on the feeling that the home gives you. Now, I spoke about the basis of this hygge movement as being focused on comfortable and cozy living. Well, I have to also add in that it's also about making sure things are in order, serves a purpose, and to create a sense of intimacy in the home.

To many, this idea of intimacy is indeed cozy and comfortable, which is why I want to focus on it as often as I can.

With this, there are so many things to take into account to ultimately produce that warm space that we call home. Let's be honest; it's much easier to prefer to walk into a room with snug blankets, comfortable chairs, soft lighting, a fire crackling, as opposed to walking into a room that is more sterile in its approach.

To help you, I'm going to go through different aspects that I feel are key to unlocking the true meaning of hygge. It's up to you to take the most important points from each section, but if you can do this and pull things together, then I'm convinced you will be able to have a home that does indeed fit in with what hygge is all about.

The Concept of Colors

I'm going to start with something that you may not have been expecting, colors.

Colors are important. In fact, they go beyond that as they are capable of providing that same relaxed and comfortable feeling in a room that we are going to keep on coming back to throughout the book.

Now, I'm not going to say that every single time you think of a color that it has to be bright. That is just not the point I'm trying to make here. Instead, dark colors can also be useful in various settings, and I'll cover both in this chapter.

The first thing I need to mention is to avoid those sharp and vibrant, in your face, colors and this applies no matter if we are talking about walls, furnishings, or anything else.

The general rule of thumb is that you should stick with those shades that are more earthy when it comes to their tone. They are regarded as being far more calming than those loud and brash tones. That's not to say that you cannot include a splash of color; it's just when it is the dominant shade that it becomes problematic.

For your walls, the Danes prefer to stick with either white or a soft gray color. Alternatively, cream could be another option. The idea here is that it will bounce the light around the room, which they love to do, so you should avoid those dark colors as they also tend to make a room feel smaller than it is.

There should also be a restriction on the number of colors that are playing a significant role in a room at any given time. Too many shades are just hard on the eyes, and this busy nature does the complete opposite to calming you down.

Monochrome or Tonal Coloring.

If you spend time examining the Danes and their approach to color, then you will quickly see that they have a tendency to go for one of two options. The first is a monochromatic approach, but this doesn't have to be as boring as it may very well sound to a number of people.

They will tend to have the same color as the predominant shade on the walls with something such as white being popular. They will then enhance their décor by using different materials, but I'll get to that in a later chapter.

The other option is known as tonal coloring. This approach means that you will be using a handful of colors, but they are all within the same shade and spectrum, so they kind of blend together quite well. This does just add some extra zing to the room, but at the same time, it avoids that problem of the colors just being overpowering. Also, we are talking about soft shades as well, but even with these more delicate shades, it all works well thanks to the other things that you will tend to end up doing within each and every room in order to complete the look.

An example of this would be the use of a range of shades of gray from the primary color on the wall to the soft furnishings. However, you are talking about shades from light to darker, so there is still enough variety without it being too overpowering.

Dark Colors in the Room.

Remember I said I would mention dark colors? Well, after reading the previous section regarding tonal colors I would hazard a guess that you were wondering where these darker colors would come into play.

As I hinted at, you should not be looking at using too many dark colors, especially in smaller rooms. They will tend to make the room both look and feel smaller, and even though that can be cozy, it is still widely frowned upon.

However, in hygge, you should ultimately do whatever makes you feel happy, and if that includes dark colors, then I say go for it. After all, when it's done correctly, it can have a rather decadent feel and in its own right that can be rather luxurious and sumptuous. If you do decide to go down that particular path, then I would stress the need for lighting and to really go over the top with the thick blankets or cushions that I'll discuss later.

Finally, just be aware of having too many dark colors together. By all means, have a dark color as a feature wall but just think about that light dancing across the room and how it will be absorbed by the dark colors.

So, I think I can perhaps sum up the use of colors in this instance by stating the following:

- Light colors are often best in rooms.

- White, off-white or soft gray tend to be the most popular.

- Light colors allow the light to bounce around the room.

- Dark colors often make the room feel smaller and are over-powering.

- Focus more on earthy tones.

- Use tonal coloring to create a sense of uniformity.

- Ultimately, do whatever makes you feel happiest with the colors you like.

But next, I'm going to move onto something else that you wouldn't have been expecting me to talk about, and that is the use of music in creating that unique atmosphere in your home.

The Use of Music to Create that Feeling

In the second chapter, I discussed the concept of creating a certain feeling and atmosphere in your home, and music can have a huge role to play in helping you to add to that feeling. Now, clearly you are going to be unable to have it playing as you walk in the door after being at work, but let's look more closely at the role it plays within the confines of hygge and the home.

First, whenever you are playing music, or however you are playing it, you need to make sure that you have good acoustics. Also, music should not be dominating to a point where people have to effectively shout to one another in order to be heard. Doing so is anti-hygge as it creates a sense of agitation and starts to really stress people out.

The type of music is also important. Obviously, it must be relaxing for you to listen to and there should be no real sense of it being all charged with energy. If something is going to make you hyper, then that's not exactly in line with just being able to chill out. However, the choice of music is entirely up to your own personal tastes, so the key is just being able to kick back and enjoy it.

Music in the Background.

In an ideal world, your music will be largely in the background. The Danes are not that keen on having it blaring out, and you should still be able to have a conversation with people without resorting to shouting and screaming to be heard. There is just no need for you to have a massive stereo system that can be heard down your street.

It should be relaxing, enjoyable, make your heart sing more than your voice and bring you comfort. It's not about having a full-on party but is there just to help you chill out. This means you should use any kind of music that appeals to you in this way. For some, it may be jazz. For others classical and so on.

Music should make you feel as if you are being wrapped up in a warm blanket and allow you just to let your mind drift off to another place far away from the stresses and strains of day to day life.

Also, music should be capable of transcending rooms. It should be able to be played virtually anywhere in your home. It should fill the room with its own type of atmosphere and generate a far better energy as a result. It must fill you with joy which is why creating your own playlists is such a good idea, so you know that there is never going to be a bad song in there.

Dealing with the Equipment.

There is something else I need to discuss regarding music, and that is dealing with the equipment that tends to come with it.

Now, if you have a stereo system with speakers and all of the cables that hang around, well that is messy, and a mess is not hygge. So, you have to think of an alternative solution if you are serious about adopting this way of life into your home.

The best method is to make sure that the items are hidden away from view when they are not in use. The Danes love the idea of a cabinet for their stereo where the speakers are closed away as it then provides a clearer appearance. Also, consider wireless speakers to solve that particular problem as it is hardly going to fit in with the minimalist approach if there are cables in clear view.

Some people will look at using Bluetooth equipment just to deal with the cable issue, and this is certainly an option I would point you towards.

A home without music at different times is actually quite dead. Music brings a vibrancy and thanks to the range of styles it is entirely possible to create different atmospheres just by the songs you play. It can lift your spirits, and it can relax you as well. With that in mind, you can see why music does indeed play such a special role within the hygge home.

Scents and the Role They Play

One thing that I have noticed on a number of occasions when individuals are attempting to incorporate this idea of hygge into their home is that they forget one thing that I see as being important, the scent.

This is not so crazy as it sounds. You just have to think about the way in which aromatherapy and essential oils are known to be very effective at changing the mood, helping you to relax, or even feeling as if you are full of energy.

So, if they can do that when you are putting essential oils on a burner, then why would they not then play a role when you are looking at things from a hygge perspective? The answer, for some, is that there are those within the hygge realm that don't believe in scents. They will focus more on unscented candles for example.

But I don't believe that approach. Why should scents be viewed as anything other than a tool that can help change the atmosphere?

Well, the answer is that they can indeed play a huge role, and it's one thing that I so desperately want to address.

To do this, I am going to encourage you to imagine a few things in your mind as you read along. In fact, let's begin by going on a journey in our mind.

You are stressed at what is going on in your life, and you cannot wait until you get home. Upon doing so, you open the door, and nothing. It's just you walking into your home.

This is hardly inspiring or relaxing, is it?

Or, how about this?

You are still in that same negative mindset as you come home. You open the door, and within minutes you have the smell of lavender weaving its way through the rooms to calm your mind. Alternatively, you use sweet orange or lemongrass as a way to uplift your mood and give you some energy. Perhaps you have a room spray that has a mixture of different essential oils that just adds life to the room as it teases and tantalizes your nose.

Surely you can see how this would be the better option out of the two?

Being Careful with the Usage.

Even though I am an advocate of using scents and aromatherapy around the home, I'm well aware that it is all too easy to overdo it, and this is not exactly helpful in its own right. In fact, if it just continually assaults your nostrils with far too many variants of smells, then it is counter-productive.

So, to continue with creating that hygge atmosphere, I tend to do the following.

First, I only have a handful of burners, and they are scattered throughout the home. I have one in the kitchen and will often use a citrus based smell to take away the odor of food. Alternatively, you can add peppermint and tea tree to water in order to help clean your kitchen, and this will also take away some of the scents.

I also tend to have another burner in the lounge. This often incorporates a range of scents depending on my mood, but it does help to really create that atmosphere, and it's wonderful to

18

have the likes of lavender in the burner sitting there wrapped up in a warm blanket reading a book in the evening.

One area that can often be overlooked with a burner or diffuser is the bathroom. This, in my opinion, is madness because the bathroom should be a place of serenity and calmness and scents will just add to that feeling. Once again, the scents can vary, but something such as rosemary or geranium while having a bath by candlelight does help to create a special something.

Also, you can throw in things such as room sprays, air fresheners, potpourri in a bowl in the hallway, scents being scattered on the carpet to freshen it up and have it smelling amazing. The list just goes on and on like crazy. Like I said, you can easily overdo it with scents, and that must be avoided at all costs.

If you are planning on adopting hygge into your home, then make scents a more central part of your approach than you may have anticipated. Trust me when I say it is going to make a difference.

Focusing on the Use of Light

When I take you on a tour through your home and examine how these different concepts can be applied on a room by room basis, you will notice that I mention light on a number of occasions.

Light is absolutely central to the home across Scandinavia, and not just Denmark. Just think of the typical Scandinavian décor – more of which in the next chapter – and how they have a preference for white, for space, and huge windows that allow natural light to flood in. The white is no coincidence. It takes the natural light that comes in and bounces it all over the room making it appear to be more spacious.

Also, there's a sense in hygge that light just does something to a room. It brings it to life and adds a certain freshness to it. This idea of freshness is also something I'll be referring to time and time again.

However, I must stress that even though natural light is important, the way in which you use subtle lighting is also key. You need to keep in mind that Denmark does spend a sizeable proportion of the winter hours in darkness. Natural light is not exactly forthcoming, so they have had to adopt different strategies whereby other forms of lighting can add a certain feeling or atmosphere to a room.

So, to make life easier, let's split things up into natural and artificial light in this chapter.

Dealing with Natural Light.

As I said, natural light adds freshness to a room. It brightens things up, and yet so many of us will spend a considerable amount of time trying to dress the window by adding curtains, or various forms of blinds to cover up aspects of the light. While this may be required at times, it's certainly not the type of thing I would recommend.

Instead, you want to be allowing as much natural light into each and every room as you can. Throw those curtains back to reveal the windows in all of their glory.

People will look at how the light floods in, the time of the day when it is at its brightest, and then often design an entire room around that light. It will influence their color schemes, where furniture is placed, and even the size of the furniture.

Taking advantage of the natural light is essential in hygge. Anything else is just so wrong, but then having natural light is not going to help you when it's dark and it gets even worse in winter when daylight is at an absolute premium. In those cases, you need to look at other options, and I'll do that next.

Other Lighting Forms.

We are going to talk about candles in the next section, so at this point, it's all about other types of lighting, and the Danes really know how to create an atmosphere in a room just by a few well-placed lights. Of course, those same lights all need to have their own purpose and be functional as there's more to it than just being purely for decoration.

First, throw out those strong light bulbs as being more subtle with light is the key. Fairy lights in dark corners is a good idea. A well-positioned lamp that adds some light to the dining table area without being overpowering. A light next to a chair so you can sit and read without straining your eyes.

It's all about planning what is going to happen in a room, where it is going to happen, and the correct lighting solutions for that need. You cannot just go and throw any old lamp in there as that doesn't always work.

Now, I accept that this could sound as if I'm telling you to have lights all over the place, but that's not the case. Rather, I'm talking about careful positioning and just putting thought into it. The entire aim is to create that cozy and comfortable atmosphere, so you can understand why the full on 100W bulb is not the best option. Look at the room carefully and decide how to get the absolute most out of it and you will be quite content with the results.

I always want to throw in another idea that does fit in with hygge and lighting, and that is using a dimmer switch. It's very easy to adjust the atmosphere and mood in a room with it being done in an instant.

Using Candles.

The Danes are known for their love of candles. In fact, they are one of the biggest purchasers of candles in the world, and it's all down to hygge. For this, they love both those that are purely for light purposes as well as those that come with a scent, and I covered the scent side of things elsewhere.

Candles are an amazing thing. Is there anything else that can create such a warm and cozy feeling than having an array of candles flickering away in a room when it's cold and dark outside? Stepping inside from that chilly wind or driving rain into a space that has a few candles just makes you feel that it is so inviting and you instantly forget everything that you just encountered.

They are, perhaps, the ultimate addition for creating a hygge atmosphere in your home.

However, this depends on how you use them because the Danes don't just throw candles all over the place; it's more subtle than that.

What you will often find when dealing with hygge is that the placement of objects is all important, and this does also apply when looking at candles. The idea is that they can be used to illuminate just aspects of the room. A dark, cold corner can immediately become so much warmer when a lit candle is placed there. Candles on top of the fireplace give that warmth as well, so don't leave them out.

I'd also recommend having candles of various sizes and styles. It just adds a bit of character and interest to a room. Also, they don't all have to be lit, and even if you are worried about wax then there are battery operated candles that will give off a flicker effect, and they can still be pretty good.

This is certainly one thing I would make sure was always in stock in my home, and I just feel that you should do the same.

How Your Decor Influences Things

I feel that talking about your décor as a follow-on chapter to the use of light makes so much sense. After all, the two go hand in hand since the amount of light can even influence the entire approach to décor that you end up going with.

However, here's something that I need to stress as being important when it comes to the décor. Choose a style and go with it. Don't mix and match various styles where one version clashes with another; it just doesn't lead to a relaxed and calming atmosphere as it comes across as a bit of a mess.

But then, do yourself a favor and stop trying to make each and every room appear as if it should be in a showroom. A golden rule of hygge is that each and every room has to reflect what makes you happy. Nothing else actually matters. If you want the minimalist approach, then go for it. If you want to have a busier style, then go for that as well just as long as you are content, and the overall atmosphere is not one that is overpowering.

I'm not telling you that you need to become some amazing interior designer. In fact, one of the best things about hygge is that there's no need for things to be perfect. The 'thrown together' look works well in this instance and even though I'm going to suggest a number of things you will ultimately do whatever makes you feel happy and comfortable in your home. It is your space, after all.

Using a Mixture of Materials.

Keeping on with the point regarding décor, you are going to want to use a combination of materials to help create that hygge feeling. The idea here is that this blend of textures is capable of adding some real interest to the room as it may otherwise be regarded as rather plain due to the tendency for the monochrome effect to become rather flat.

If you check out Scandinavian homes, then they will use natural fabrics, have a mixture of different woods of various shades, thick carpets or rugs, in other words, it is a very tactile thing. They will also use metal at various times as well, but it's not as industrial as it may sound.

They tend to include rather warm materials as well, since this is clearly going to add to that cozy feeling you are trying to achieve, and I would strongly recommend that you do the same. A wool blanket draped over a chair that you can sit and read a book under a soft light is the epitome of hygge. That sheepskin rug on the floor – it doesn't have to be real sheepskin – just adds that layer of warmth and comfort on an otherwise barren floor. Fluffy cushions or mixing and matching different sizes and materials can also work well.

However, here's a point I need to mention, and it's to do with the color. You should try to keep the colors of the materials within the same spectrum of tonal colors that you are using elsewhere. There should be no sense of them clashing since this extra 'noise' is often not exactly relaxing.

Thinking About the Walls.

You will be able to come up with countless ideas for the floor that are in keeping with the hygge concept, but what about the walls? Well, there are still several things that you can do that are capable of completely transforming a room. Of course, it's up to you as to which ones appeal the most.

For some, it is a luxurious wallpaper even as a feature wall. Embossed and even with a touch of velvet coming from it can just give that warmth. Wall lights casting shadows over the walls can also bring them to life, and then there's artwork or personal photographs in elaborate and ornate frames.

How about wall decals to break up a large blank space? They are easy to apply, and there are a whole host of designs that can be incorporated so perhaps check them out to see if anything fits in with the theme that you are going for.

In other words, the walls do not have to be boring, far from it.

Going with a Theme.

Often, people will go for some kind of theme with the décor, especially in the kitchen and bathroom where you will have fruits and vegetables on the walls or seashells all over the place. To be honest, you are better going for a theme that is a bit toned down and more serene. It's fine to have some fun in rooms, but it is often the case that people go over the top with this and that in itself can become rather distracting.

Instead, I would recommend that you keep things relatively simple and play around with a few key items that add your own personal touch to a room. Remember, it is still something that is personal to you, so you have to make sure that it's not completely sterile of the kind of things that tells the story as to the kind of person that you are.

Don't Forget Your Furniture

Furniture does have a major role to play in this particular approach to a comfortable home. However, as with everything else, there are a number of things that you just can or cannot do.

First, I want to address something that is important.

There's a need for you to assess if each item of furniture that you own has a role to play, or is it just effectively gathering up dust? You see, in the chapter that follows, I'm going to discuss the issue of clutter and how it is anti-hygge. Of course, furniture can also be seen as clutter, but I follow a good general rule of thumb to help with this.

If you have a small room with limited space, then generally go for smaller pieces of furniture. For example, in a small lounge, you should consider small nesting tables rather than a large coffee table that just dominates the main part of the floor space. The reason for this approach is simply because those individuals that have adopted hygge into their life will often go by the mantra that less is more. Also, when you are working in a small space and using smaller items of furniture, it means you can create a wider range of atmospheres and play around with their positioning, which is always a bonus.

How to Make Sense of Your Furniture.

The way in which the idea of furniture is incorporated into hygge is quite straightforward.

There's no point in having furniture just for the sake of owning it. Furniture is there to be used, and you should have no problem in being able to do so. For example, a dining table that is covered in clutter or pushed into a corner whereby it becomes unusable is completely pointless. Furniture that is damaged in some way such as the leg on a chair being unsteady or a shelf in a cupboard being broken is also pointless.

Furthermore, the size of your furniture in relation to the dimensions of the room also has to be examined. A coffee table that takes up too much floor space in your lounge making it tricky to get around it should be moved. A TV screen that is too large sitting on an item of furniture that is too high resulting in light being blocked out has to be moved.

I hope that I'm putting across the idea that this is all to do with functionality and to make sure that everything has its place. Yes, that family heirloom may be precious, but it needs to have its own correct spot rather than just being pushed into a corner.

You must be honest with your appraisal of the furniture that can fit into a room quite comfortably. A hygge room is pretty unique in that it wants to create that sense of being cozy and often people will think of that as being quite enclosed, and yet they love space. In the case of furniture, it is the space that is the important part because if you have too many items in a room and are constantly banging into things, then that is hardly going to create a serene and calm atmosphere.

Choosing the Correct Items.

I personally put probably too much thought into the items that are in a room. I am a stickler for measurements as well because you must be able to use everything for the purpose that it was intended for and that cannot be done if you effectively have furniture piled up on top of each other.

Before putting an item of furniture into a room, you need to really think about its use and don't just run out and buy something because it is on sale. It will only be a bargain if it is actually something that you need because if that's not the case, then you are wasting cash.

Will you use it? How will you use it? Does it fit in with the rest of the room? Do you need to throw something out to make space for it? All of these questions are important simply because you need to be fully aware of the function of a piece of furniture before you go ahead and get it.

The Style.

Aside from choosing the correct items and being aware of its use, you need to also think about the style of the furniture along with the material that it is built from. This is something that does change according to tastes as they do chop and change on a regular basis.

Forget the idea that everything has to match, believe me, that this is not the case. However, at the same time, you don't want to have too many clashes since this can be rather disconcerting. For me, the most important thing is that it fits in and overall it can tie in with the design that you are actually looking for at this point.

Remember to Upcycle.

The final point I'm going to discuss regarding furniture is the idea of upcycling. This is something that the Danes love to do as it means you are bringing in an old piece of furniture that has so much character and life followed by then giving it a brand new lease of life.

This approach is seen as being rather fulfilling, and it's easy to see why. The actual process of stripping it down, painting it, changing its appearance and then seeing the finished product is capable of providing you with a real sense of achievement.

Also, there is no need for the item to be perfect. It's not about that. Instead, it's about having something special to you and an item that is capable of bringing you joy and happiness. In your eyes, it is perfect even if the edges are ragged and it's not all painted perfectly.

In addition, taking an old item and changing its purpose is another idea that is straight out of the hygge handbook. Just because something appears to have come to the end of its use does not mean that it needs to be thrown out. It may just need a few alterations, and it will be able to last you for a number of years.

Clutter and Having its Place

If I can take you back to the Scandinavian style of home in order to discuss the idea of dealing with clutter and everything having its place in each and every room.

Too often, we end up with all of these items around us that just take up space, and that's a problem. It's hardly going to help us to create that harmonious feeling that we are seeking, is it?

So, what I need you to do is to address the issue, and it's not always going to be an easy thing to do. In fact, dealing with clutter and working through those objects that we may end up throwing away is tough. However, there is a hygge way of doing this as well, and I'm going to tell you all about it.

With hygge, there is a sense of things being done in an orderly manner. Also, you need to do things with a clear mind and not consumed by stress and anxiety, or feeling that something has to be done in world record time.

That just does not work, and it increases the chances of you doing something that you later regret.

The Problem with Clutter.

Clutter is indeed a problem. Us humans appear to have evolved to a point where we find it amazingly easy to accumulate 'stuff' even to the stage where we cannot remember we have things or why we got them in the first place.

It is said that this build-up of clutter is representative of a build-up of thoughts and chaos in our mind, and it does not exactly fit in well with our idea of how to be relaxed about our home.

So, we need to deal with it before the stress of all of these objects around us just gets too much for our brains to comprehend.

To deal with this, you need to be quite hard on yourself. There's a very real need for you to work out what is staying and what is going. Do you use it? Is it merely decorative, and pretty pointless if we are being honest? Does it have sentimental value and that's why you are keeping it?

Now, I'm certainly not telling you to go and throw everything out until you are left with the absolute bare minimum. I'm also certainly not instructing you to dispose of those sentimental items. That would be horrible.

Instead, here's what I'm telling you to do.

1. Sort things out room by room.

We have the ability to gather clutter in various rooms, so you need to be methodical. Go through each room and decide on the items you have not even touched for a number of months because it's more than likely to be the case that those items can go. Also, things that are broken can be disposed of, and of course there will be items that you either need to keep, or just want to keep.

2. Be brutal.

It's important to be quite brutal when you are dealing with clutter. Too often we can be drawn in by spending too much time thinking about an item. Now, I'm not saying that you have to throw out everything that has sentimental value as that's not the case. Instead, if you have more than one of something and you never use both, then throw one out. It's as easy as that.

3. Pass things on.

You don't have to throw everything out especially when you are talking about something that is still in perfect working order. By the rules of hygge, you should be seeking to pass those things onto people that will benefit from them and be able to enjoy them. This can be done by donating to a charity or, alternatively, giving it to someone you know and who will cherish and treasure whatever it is that you own.

Also, when you do pass things on, it might sound crazy but give it thanks for the role it played in your life. It served a purpose, whatever that purpose may be, for some time and it's just a case that its time has passed.

Dealing with the Clutter.

There's a reason why you go to Ikea, as an example, and become amazed at the innovative storage solutions that are available. That reason is entirely down to hygge, and it leads to people still being able to keep various items, but they have their place and are put away so that they do not make the room appear too busy.

It also fits in with the way in which a hygge home tends to hate large and bulky pieces of furniture, so the clever items are always going to be a winner.

Remember, furniture is also clutter, and this is a mistake that people will often make. They look at just the small items that are lying around and think that if they clear them away, then everything will be great, and it will. However, if you still have those large items hanging around, then you have only partly solved the problem.

In my case, I start with the larger items and work my way down. It's amazing how quickly you work through it with this method, and the outcome is that you will have a room that is indeed clutter free.

The Advantages of Dealing with Clutter.

I admit that some people may struggle with the clutter issue, but perhaps by mentioning the advantages that come with actively tackling it, you will come to the realization that tackle it – you must.

First, the obvious.

If clutter, in an object sense, stresses out your mind due to an inability to find things, know where to put them, or your home looking rather unkempt, then clearing it does the opposite. Yep, your mind becomes free allowing you to enjoy more things without all of this interference going on. A reduction in stress makes hygge all seem worthwhile.

Remember, not having clutter on display leads to a far more serene space which is something you need to be aiming for.

Another advantage is that it becomes easier for you to see everything that you own. How often do you decide to have a good old clear-out only to uncover a whole host of things that you never even knew existed? Suddenly, if you work through everything that you own and decide what can stay and what should go, then this no longer becomes a problem.

Imagine just being able to find what you want pretty much in an instant rather than rummaging through everything. Imagine how your stress levels would drop as a direct result of all of that.

Finally, when you own fewer items, it means that everything can indeed have its place and for there to be a sense of order in your home. Disorder is stress inducing. Order is stress reducing. Now, I know that for some people dealing with this clutter is going to be a massive job, and you are probably stressing out about it right now, so I would recommend just doing one room at a time and don't move on until you are quite content with that space.

When you tackle this methodically, which in itself is very much in line with hygge, then it's amazing how quickly you can get through everything that you need to do.

The Concept of Space and Arrangement.

Space is important in hygge, and it's often the case that we just don't have enough of it. This is due to our own personal overindulgence leading to that build-up of clutter that we have just discussed. Keep on doing it, and you will feel smothered and that is a rather uncomfortable state of affairs to be in.

Of course, after you have removed the clutter then you will have a better understanding of the space that you have available, so you need to do that first.

This is where planning comes into it, and it's certainly something that the Danes appear to excel at.

There is a very real need for you to be able to move around a room and get to everything. Plugging in those appliances should not be difficult. Switching on that light or lighting those candles should be equally as easy.

Cleaning should be a breeze thanks to the clutter being removed, so your home is going to be fresher, and with the perfect arrangement, the entire job can be done in half the time.

To create space, I would tell you to avoid those impulse buys. Yes, it might be a bargain, but it could completely throw out the equilibrium of the room. Also, don't think that things can all be pushed to the edges of the room as that's not what it's all about either.

A hygge room must flow. It must work in the way it is intended, and you should not be banging into things. It really is as simple as that.

Those Little Touches

Before I start to take you through the home and determining how you can implement the various points I've discussed above, I just need to run over something that I would like to refer to as 'those little touches.'

You see, throughout the time I've spent adopting the practices of hygge into my own life and home, I've come to realize that often it is indeed those little touches that can just make a huge difference to the overall feel of not just a room, but your home in general. Often, subtle changes can have the biggest impact, and that is pretty amazing.

So, what exactly do I mean by the idea of these little touches? Well, I'm referring to a number of important points.

1. Small Items are Useful.

When I mention small items, I'm referring to objects such as photographs, ornaments with a story to tell, or anything else that can mean something as well as be a conversation starter. This is a wonderful side to hygge in that they can break the ice and often lead to a wonderful evening, and all within the confines of your own home.

2. Little Touches Can Make You Happy.

I hope that you have not got to this point and come to some conclusion that you need to revamp your entire home as that's not the case. Instead, even though I'm giving you a series of tips, you have to remember that you are decorating your home so it should be something you like.

Those little touches will make your home feel happy, and that is the most important thing of all. Let's be honest; you don't want to come home and feel any discontent at what is awaiting you. Your home is your sanctuary as I said earlier, and these little touches can help you to really achieve that.

3. Don't Leave Broken Things.

You know how earlier on I spoke about clutter and not having things lying around? Well, I'd also throw broken items into the same equation. If it is broken and cannot be fixed, then get rid of it. The item is just taking up space and getting in your way. It serves no purpose now, and if this is the case, then you are not following the concept of hygge too closely.

The important part here is whether or not they can be fixed. By all means, give it a go as even that can be quite peaceful and healing in its own way. However, if it starts to stress you out, then it has to go but when you throw something out, make sure you thank it for the role it once played and that you enjoyed it.

I accept that I've covered an array of points and issues and it may be rather confusing for those that are new to hygge and what it's all about. However, I'm going to be quite clever here and take you step by step even though this is also going to include so many aspects of hygge that have already been covered.

The good news is you will be able to start to really see them being put into action, which just makes life so much easier.

Creating a Hyggekrog

As a short aside, I'm going to throw in something that is often overlooked, and yet, it can make such a huge difference to the way you feel about your home. I'm talking about you creating something called a hyggekrog, but you might know it better as a snug.

This doesn't mean that you need to turn an entire room into a snug as that's not the case. Instead, I'm talking about taking just a corner of a room and converting it into this secluded spot that is just going to be your refuge even within your home.

The way you achieve this is entirely up to you, but there are certain things that you need to consider for it to be a success.

Try to Get a View.

In an ideal world, your hyggekrog should have some kind of a view out to nature. If that's not possible, then you need to try to create a view, and I'll help you out with that later.

This is where having a window seat is perfect. However, if you don't have one, then a comfortable chair looking out of the window will also suffice.

When it comes to making a view, then have some amazing photographs in ornate frames for you to look at or some kind of wall art. The idea is that you can effectively lose yourself in what you are looking at as this is going to rather quickly help to calm the mind.

Get Comfortable.

Your snug should be, well, snug. This cozy feeling can be achieved in a number of different ways, and it's all up to you as to which ones are more suitable for your own personal tastes. In my case, I like to make sure that cushions are both comfortable as well as supportive and that there is a cozy throw or blanket there just to keep things warm.

I'd also strongly recommend having layers of comfortable furnishings. This is supposed to be almost over the top cozy; it is a snug, after all, so don't be afraid to have a range of cushions and even a choice of throws or blankets of varying degrees of warmth.

Oh, and if you have a wooden floor in the room where your snug is located, then I'd add a nice warm rug in the area just to give your feet something soft and warm.

Remember the Light.

Light can be a major influencing factor in your snug and obviously if you have a view, then there will be a considerable amount of natural light flowing in. But then, this restricts your ability to use the snug in those darker hours, and that would be a shame.

So, I'd have a couple of options ready to go when it comes to light in your snug. First, forget about having a main source of light as that's just too overpowering. Instead, candles can be perfect, but if you are planning on using your snug as a reading space, then a light perfectly positioned next to the chair to allow you to do so will be suitable.

Understand its Use.

I feel that there is no point in having a hyggekrog if you are unsure as to how you will be using it. Imagine putting in all of that effort, and it just sits there barren.

There are so many uses if you stop and put your mind to it, but one thing I would stress is that you should not use it for playing video games even on your smartphone. The only electronics I would allow would be a Kindle for reading a book, although the real thing is better, or an MP3 player to listen to music.

This snug should be a spot where there is peace and quiet. You might even want to listen to some music, through headphones clearly, as you just chill out and that is going to add to the overall feeling that you are striving for. It should be serene and feel like your own personal cocoon even within the home like a den in the back garden but this time for adults.

This spot is popular in Danish homes. It allows them to get away from everything and even the children are trained to know that this is a quiet spot and for the person that is in there to be left alone. It allows you to recharge your batteries, and perhaps you even end up having a nap in your snug because that is also fine.

The decoration is entirely up to you. After all, this is your snug, and the only advice I would give is to make it as comfortable as possible. Find the thickest rug you have ever seen in your life. Rich, velvet curtains to add that touch of luxury. Cushions that are voluptuous. Blankets or throws that can be wrapped around yourself time and time again. If possible, make a window seat and have the option of closing off the area with a curtain or a folding screen to give privacy.

The choice is entirely up to you, but as you can see, there are a number of things to go on.

That being said, we have looked extensively at different things that you should focus on including color, light, and space to name just a few. I need to move things on and try to show you those things in action, and the best way to do that is by taking you through your home. Well, a made up home since I have no idea what your own one is like.

Starting Outside the Home

I have this aim of taking you through your home in what I feel is a logical manner. To me, this makes so much sense as it should just make everything so much easier for you to follow. Now, throughout the chapters that are about to come, I'm going to make reference to a number of the points that I mentioned earlier. As you will see, the way in which they can be incorporated into the home will vary from room to room, but the end result will hopefully be the same. A home that is not only hygge at its best, but also one that is comfortable and is loved by you and your family.

With that in mind, I'm going to kick things off by starting with the outside of your home because even if you live in an apartment block rather than having a driveway or path, then so many aspects of hygge can still be applied.

It's All About the Approach.

I want you to picture these two different scenarios and for you to then determine which one sounds best.

First, you walk towards your home, and it's dark as it is in the evening. Your front door is in the shadows, it may be raining, and the rain is hitting against your door. Plants nearby are unruly and seem to be completely taking over the entire space.

Or.

You walk towards your home; it's still dark and raining. However, this time it's different. This time, lights are scattered throughout the plants that line the driveway or path. There is a porch at the front of your door. It protects it from the rain. A light glows underneath giving a warm feeling to it all. There may be an ornamental style plant beside the door if there's space and a mat on the ground for you to wipe your feet on but which also serves a purpose as a way to welcome you home.

Out of both scenarios, there is really only one that is capable of adding a certain sense of warmth to your heart. There's only one that will make you feel happier about coming home as you are not then enshrouded by gloom while you battle the elements just to enter your front door.

But, I want to take it further so, for this moment, I want to focus on a setting for those individuals that also have a garden, no matter how big or small. For those that live in an apartment block, I'll come back to you shortly as there are still so many things that you can do in accordance with the concept of hygge.

The Garden Approach.

I'm calling this the garden approach, and I'm going to move to both front and back as there are different ideas that can be applied to each area. No matter which one we are discussing, I must stress that throughout it all you need to be aware of what you will be looking at from inside your home. This is important simply because you want to be able to get the same warm, comforting feeling no matter if you are inside or outside as both should work in tandem.

Let's start things off with the front garden.

1. Keeping it Tidy.

A huge part of hygge is that things are organized, they have their place, and you do not have any clutter, and the exact same thing applies even in the garden. Those jobs that you keep putting off simply because you feel you do not have the time have to be completed. Just as clutter is an issue on the inside, the same goes for the outside.

Mow lawns, trim plants, pick up leaves, wash the driveway, the list is going to go on and on, but it just makes everything feel that bit better.

2. Remember Lights.

You don't want to have the lead up to your home being in the dark, so garden lights are an absolute must. You may decide to have one attached to the building itself with a movement sensor so it comes on automatically or you might decide to go down an alternative path.

There are actually so many outdoor light options from solar powered lamps to battery operated lights of all shapes and sizes. They can line the path as lanterns. They can be placed in trees and bushes to add life to them. Be as adventurous and crazy as you want with lights as they just make the outside of your home more inviting.

3. Plants, Plants, and Plants.

Hygge involves nature, so it makes sense that plants play a huge part in the garden. The idea of just some tarred yard with a wall is so plain and boring that if the Danes adopted that approach, they would never have been the happiest nation alive.

Plants bring so much life to the area. They are also nice to look at from the inside. I would advise getting some specialist advice if you are unsure as to what works in your area. You don't need to have a jungle, and you do have to learn how to look after them as well, but don't be boring and just have one or two pots as that is just not going to work.

4. Remember Maintenance.

Even though hygge is not about being perfect, you should look at mending that broken wooden fence, painting the metal railings, painting the house if that is what is required just so nothing looks tired and worn. Just as you have pride on the inside, the same must apply to the outside.

The Back Garden and Hygge.

I'm going to discuss several important factors regarding your back garden or yard, and I strongly suggest that you try to incorporate them wherever possible. The back garden is the place where we will socialize more or just laze around in the sun as it is generally more private. As it has a different function, it means we can apply some different concepts.

1. Have a Cozy Option Outside.

You will learn how feeling cozy is a huge part of hygge as you progress through this book. This cozy feeling is something that I would implore you to take advantage of even with your back yard, and there are various ways to achieve this.

Personally, I would look at purchasing a fire pit or brazier. A chimenea could be another alternative or a patio heater powered by a gas cylinder is yet another option.

The entire idea is to make sure that you still feel comfortable even in the evening when the temperature has dropped slightly. Also, the crackle of the fire can be soothing, and depending upon which option you go for there is also the possibility of you toasting some marshmallows while you relax.

Just because you are outdoors does not mean you can forget about being cozy. It just doesn't work like that.

2. Dealing with Seating.

Aside from a cozy fire, having the correct seating will also add to your comfort levels. There are so many options that there will be something perfect for you no matter if we are talking about a full patio set or a love seat or even a hammock. It's about whatever works for you in the space you have available as well as your budget.

3. Remember the Blankets.

You should have a ready supply of blankets for sitting outside in an evening especially when the sun goes down. There's no reason why your garden should be off limits just because it has got colder, so those warm blankets beside the warm fire make for that complete hygge experience.

Plan for Autumn and Winter.

Depending on where you live, there's every chance that you will have a certain level of disdain for the colder months simply because your outdoor space looks rather derelict and barren. Well, that doesn't have to be the case thanks to hygge, but it does require some planning ahead on your part.

As daylight hours can be in short supply for some people, it's important to keep this in mind when looking at your lighting options that provide a sense of life even in those dark corners. After all, it becomes pointless for you to use solar powered lighting when there are insufficient levels of solar power, to begin with.

But that doesn't mean that you have to give up with lighting even in these darker months.

I would suggest that you look at having some mains powered lights or, if you are prepared to keep on changing them, there are battery powered options out there. Keep that fire burning and double up on those blankets and your garden is still going to be used. The Danes get it pretty cold, and they can still do it.

Thinking Ahead with Planting.

Another key area to think about for the sake of the colder months is the planting. I feel that it is a waste of time focusing on plants that effectively go into hibernation during these darker times. Their foliage falls off, and everything just looks as if it is dead, and that is hardly in keeping with hygge.

However, you clearly do not have to go that way. There is a whole host of alternative options out there for you to at least consider.

My own personal approach is to look for a mixture of plants. Some will stay green throughout the year, and I strive to have a variety of shades of green and yellow just to break things up. Also, there are a number of plants that look spectacular in autumn with the shades of deep red, orange, yellow, and other strongly autumnal colors.

For inspiration, perhaps consider these plants.

- Acer tree: Has a gorgeous dark red color in autumn.

- Fothergilla gardenii: Will produce leaves that are red and deep orange in autumn.

- Winterberry: Festooned with rich red berries that also attract birds in winter.

- Cornus kousa: Aside from the flowers, the leaves turn a mixture of yellow and orange.

Remembering the Sun.

Even during those winter months, I still recommend you getting out into the sun even if it's just for 10 minutes before you need to dash back inside. Of course, you should be clever and wrap up warm and have a hot drink with you so that it's more bearable.

Even with this, there is some forward planning on your part so you can indeed take advantage of what little sun there may be. For example, are you aware of the part of your garden that tends to get the sun for the longest part of the day in winter? If not, then I'd find out because that spot will become your focal point in winter.

Get a comfortable garden chair, or if you have a summer house then try to position it where it will still be flooded with light even in the winter. If you then have snug blankets in your summer house and that cushioned chair, then these brief moments outdoors in the winter are far more pleasant.

For those in an Apartment.

I'm jumping back a bit to the start of this chapter for those individuals that live in an apartment. You still have a front door, and there's no reason why you cannot make it as inviting as you can even though you don't have the garden aspect.

For this, I would recommend making sure you have a good welcoming mat at your front door. The space outside should be kept clean at all times as well. You can also add your number and get one made out of metal and is a bit more ornate as that will work better. A couple of plastic plants in pots with one either side of the door can also make a difference. Finally, make sure that the lights leading up to your apartment are in working order as you hardly want to get there in the dark.

As you can see, there are various things you are able to do leading up to your home, but then it is really on the inside where the magic is going to happen.

The Entrance Hallway

Switching back to the house, we find ourselves opening the front door and stepping inside. Now, you would be quite correct in expecting there to be a need for this space to be perfect from the point of view of an individual that is following hygge.

For me, the entrance hallway has the ability just to make you feel so glad that you are home. However, this is only the case when it is warm and inviting rather than the opposite.

So, what kind of things would I recommend that fit in with this Danish concept? Well, there's a few key points that you just cannot avoid, and believe me when I say that they make a huge difference.

Remember that your aim is to create something that is warm and comforting. Just imagine the difference it makes when you step in from the cold or the rain to then be faced with a more tranquil and serene setting that is the hallway equivalent of a mug of hot cocoa in front of a log fire.

In my case, there were several key things I had to include.

First, a place to keep my shoes and an umbrella stand. It is just practical, or you have rainwater running all over the place and being able to take your shoes off and store them somewhere stops you dragging mud all over the house.

I also had a soft light that helped to create that more relaxed atmosphere. I would tend to have it on so it could come through the glass in the upper part of the door as this created that glow as I approached. It's amazing how something as simple as that makes a difference.

Also, I had heating next to the door as it does get a bit cold here and there's nothing better than walking in and being hit by the warmth. It lifts your spirits immediately as does a nice room scent that is warm and inviting.

Oh, and here is a little tip straight out of Denmark for the hallway. A basket full of thick, warm and snug socks. Take your shoes off and slip a pair of socks on instead. They are so comfortable, and it just sets you up perfectly for the relaxation that is ahead of you.

Finally, you want to make sure that you have somewhere to hang your coat, scarf, or whatever and it shouldn't be laden down with remnants from excursions gone by. This in itself is clutter, so don't do it.

The entire idea here is just to create a welcoming space and one that you are glad to see. It doesn't take much on your part, but the difference it makes is huge.

Hygge and the Lounge

If we step in off the hallway, then we can enter the lounge, and this is a space where hygge can really make a huge difference considering the amount of time we tend to spend in this particular room.

Now, I'm going to have to make a bit of a presumption here, and that is going to be regarding the objects or features that will tend to be in this room. I'm going to hazard a guess that there are a fireplace and seating arrangements. Hopefully, you have a nice enough view from the window, but there will also be a series of lamps in different parts of the room. There is also a pretty good chance that you have some kind of rug or warm carpet on the floor.

So, why am I telling you this? Well, it's all connected to the way in which you need to approach this room when it comes to incorporating the concepts of hygge into the layout, use, or design.

First, I want you to think for a moment about what you do in the lounge. Do you watch TV? Read a book? Entertain guests there for a few drinks and a chat?

No matter what it is, we need to make sure that the room itself is correctly set up to fit in with this idealistic way of comfortable living.

1. Look at the Features that Cannot Be Moved.

I want you to look at the features that cannot be moved as you have to work around them. You must decide how much light comes in at different periods of the day. You need to know how people can benefit from the fireplace without it really favoring some over others. If there is a staircase, then how does it work with under the stairs and is this the perfect spot for something else?

Start off with those features and then work your way down. It does make it easier.

2. Decor and Furniture.

I want you to go back to the earlier sections regarding décor and furniture as they are rather important. For furniture, start off with the large pieces such as the sofa and get the positioning correct. Then, see the space that is left when you add in the television, stereo system, and anything else that you feel has to go in there.

Once you have an understanding of how busy the room is going to be, you can think of the décor. Remember and stick with tonal colors throughout the room.

3. The Lights.

For fear of repeating myself, I'll try and discuss this in a different way.

I feel that the lounge should have soft lighting with fairy lights, small table lamps with low power bulbs, and candles are important. Think about where you may like to read a book and position a lamp accordingly, so you don't have to strain your eyes. Use soft lights to highlight corners that would otherwise be dark and to bring them to life. Candles on the fireplace or coffee table may sound obvious, but they are often missed.

4. Keep it Practical and Usable.

Everything should be achieved with ease. The fire should be lit without any difficulties. If you are having a coffee, then a table should be at hand to allow you to rest your mug. You should know where the various controls are kept, and they should be returned there. People should be positioned so they can see one another and chat without having to move and strain themselves.

There should be nothing difficult here. Everything should be easy.

5. Those Hygge Touches.

Finally, those touches that just create that atmosphere. That warm rug I've mentioned in front of the fire. A variety of cushions that make sitting more comfortable. Throws and blankets you just want to hug and hold onto. A room scent that is relaxing and calming. Soft music in the background. Perhaps even a crackling fire if that is what you have at your disposal.

To be honest, anything that is not sterile and is not just focused on the television or playing video games.

Hygge and the Bathroom

We cannot go ahead and leave the bathroom free of all of this approach to providing yourself with a comfortable home in which to live. After all, the bathroom is supposed to be a room where we can pamper ourselves and end up feeling pretty good about things, so it does have a very important role to play.

Now, there is one thing that I need to do, and that is split this particular chapter into two sections. The reason for this approach is because of the difference it makes if you have a bathroom window since natural light plays a huge role in hygge. However, even if you don't have a window, all is not lost. It simply means you have to be clever in your approach, but I'll help you with that as well.

One thing that is extremely popular within hygge is creating a bathroom that is something close to the concept of a spa. Now, you are probably not going to be lucky enough to have your own sauna or anything like that, but there are little touches that you can do that will make a huge difference.

Light in the Bathroom.

Light in the bathroom comes from either the window or artificial lights, and I do recommend that you make full use of it all. Of course, there's nothing better than a soak in the bath by candlelight in the evening, so that's hardly news to you.

But we are looking at taking things further. Why should that idea of the candlelit bath only be done on a special occasion or as some kind of treat to yourself? Surely it's best if that is the kind of experience that you have on a regular basis? Well, that is why hygge works so well. Hygge allows you to do that without too much hassle.

For the light, I would make sure that there are few obstructions in the way of the natural light coming into the room. I'll mention how the colors and furniture can also help later, but don't go ahead and put all kinds of covers on the window for your privacy. Instead, the correct glass will make a difference and still allow the light to flood in.

With alternative lighting, then I would say that you should include several different options. Long candles in decorative holders will cast a wonderfully warm glow, and position them around the room. You should also look at having a dimmer switch for the main light, or even include some battery operated fairy lights that will provide you with a relatively low level of light, but still enough to create that cozy atmosphere.

Accessories in the Bathroom and Adding Hygge.

To really go all out with the hygge approach, you need to have a fluffy robe ready and waiting for you after you shower. A thick bathmat to step out onto is another essential. The room also cannot be cold, so have adequate heating in there if that is what is required. Some people may also bring some music into their bathroom to just help add to the atmosphere, and that's certainly something that I would push you into considering.

Then there is clutter. I mentioned it in an earlier chapter, but the bathroom appears to be a particular area where there is a major problem with clutter. How quickly can you ultimately build up a collection of different lotions, soaps, shampoo, the list goes on and on.

You need to have adequate storage and also cut back on the things you own. Storage should be closed away rather than things being put into boxes and on top of cabinets as that is still clutter and messy to look at.

It can also be useful for you to look at buying a burner so you can have some essential oils going in your bathroom as well. This will add to the overall feeling and atmosphere and just help to add to that spa feeling. The same can be said with your towels which should be soft and kept on a heater of some kind, so they are nice and warm for you to then wrap yourself up in once you step out of the bath.

As you can see, I'm not talking about something that is out of the ordinary when it comes to turning your bathroom into a spa. It does take a bit of work, but considering the time we spend in this room, it's worth putting in the effort to create something that is just so relaxing and comforting.

Do yourself a favor and just remember these points for the bathroom.

• Keep the décor classy and using those tonal colors.

• Ditch the quirky shells and decorative toilet seat as it just doesn't work.

•	Get rid of most of the bottles and lotions you have gathered together.

•	Have a towel warmer as it makes a big difference.

•	Fluffy and warm robes are perfect.

•	Your bathmat should be luxurious and not just flat and practical.

•	Remember a diffuser or burner will add something to the room.

•	Use candles and fairy lights at times rather than the harsh main light.

Hygge and the Kitchen

You know how there is the idea that the kitchen is the heart of the home, well that's something that I really do go along with especially when seeking to adopt the concept of hygge.

Now, if I'm going to stay strictly within the confines of hygge, then I need to make something clear. When you are in the kitchen cooking, it has to be a joyous occasion. You should seek to use fresh ingredients, and just enjoy the entire process from start to finish. The very idea of just getting something and throwing it in the microwave to heat it up is horrific, and it's certainly not in keeping with what we are hoping to achieve.

Considering the role that food plays in entertaining, which is also a huge part of hygge, you would be quite correct in expecting the kitchen to require its own particular makeover.

The Importance of Scents.

There is nothing that the Danes love more than to have the smell of something baking in the oven floating not only through the kitchen, but also other rooms in the home. The same can be said with some dish cooking away leading to the nostrils of any individual in the vicinity being assaulted with their stomach following along in close succession.

Scents play such an important role in hygge that you just should not allow the kitchen to be cold and dead. It needs to have something cooking away in it to bring that particular sense to life.

At the same time, there should be freshness in the kitchen. Fresh fruit in a bowl. Fresh bread (and if you can make it yourself then that is even better) is always going to be a good idea. Vegetables, coffee sitting there all ready for you to drink with the smell of it being freshly brewed just emanating from the kitchen.

You can easily imagine these things without too many problems. In fact, I would guess that a number of you will have smiled at the thoughts of those smells and you are nodding your head in agreement as to how comforting they can be. So, if they are comforting for you, then make sure you incorporate them into your kitchen.

Storage is Key.

It is perhaps not a huge surprise to discover that I view storage in the kitchen as being high on the list of things to do. Worktops are often kept clear of as many gadgets as possible, so making use of every square inch of storage is essential.

Oh, a mixture of wooden tops and white cabinets is perfect, although I'll let you get away with off-white, for that hygge feeling. The position of them should also be in such a way that there is no stretching to get something. Remember, hygge is all about the ease of things, and that extends to picking up that mug to make your coffee.

Lighting.

Hygge lighting in the kitchen can take on various forms. Lights under kitchen cabinets shining down onto a glossy worktop is perfect, but only if they are soft lights. A good strong light near the cooker is also important to allow you to keep an eye on things, but it's best if this is a single light rather than allowing it to dominate the room.

Consider Metal.

Metal can work in a kitchen, but I would tend to veer towards softer tones, so a dulled down copper faucet or pans would work well. However, I'm only talking about splashes rather than anything else so it should never dominate.

Those Other Hygge Touches.

To finish off the kitchen, I have a few other ideas that are easy to implement.

First, consider growing your own herbs and have them by the window. It adds some life to the kitchen, and it just gives a better energy that there is something fresh there. Also, cut back on those fancy gadgets as they just take up space especially when you end up hardly using them.

Use soft colors and then just throw in some splashes of something else that is a bit brighter and more cheerful. It creates a vibe, and at the same time, you still have a very Scandinavian and welcoming kitchen.

Hygge and the Dining Room

If your home has a dining room, then there are a number of things that you can incorporate into the room that is in accordance with the overall feeling that we are trying to achieve.

Now, entertaining friends and family with everybody having an amazing time is a central part of hygge, so clearly, the dining room is a spot in your home where this can all really come together. In fact, this is a spot where I would spend time trying to include several of the things I mentioned earlier to help build on that feeling, and you will understand why I am focusing on them shortly.

The Dining Table.

For some, this may sound like a lot of work, but the way in which the dining table is setup should also follow certain rules when it comes to hygge.

There is a real feeling of precision at all times. Cups sit on saucers. The correct cutlery in the correct places. The overall table setting is exact where nothing is out of place. The table itself is not too large that people have to shout to one another in order to be heard. It is a place where conversation can happen naturally and without much ado.

Chairs should be comfortable and allow people to sit there idly for hours just talking to one another. There should also be space to move around the table without having to squeeze on past, but that comes down to the choice of furniture and how it fits into the space that is available.

The Decor of the Room.

The décor of the room is going to depend on one major thing, the light source. Now, some people have little light getting into the room aside from artificial lighting, but that is something that you need to get just right for it to be effective.

The light in this instance should be strong enough that everyone can see what they are eating along with seeing one another, but not too bright that it's blinding. Candles will be a wonderful addition, but soft lights suspended from the ceiling are the preferred option in most cases. It just helps with casting the correct amount of light over the room.

If you find that the room is quite small and has little natural light, then white colors would be the order of the day. In fact, white or off-white along with wooden furniture is a classical mix, and it is one that is in keeping with the overall Scandinavian feel that you will be looking for.

Thisis a place to dine and entertain. People should not be falling over one another, and there should be such a relaxed atmosphere at all times. Keep the space relatively clear of furniture apart from the essentials and focus on the comfort of the chairs and the ease with which people can chat to one another rather than worrying about plush rugs or anything else.

Hygge and the Bedroom

It's no surprise that hygge should play a huge role in how you design your bedroom because where else do you want to be as relaxed and as comfortable as possible in your home?

This is a room where the atmosphere and feeling that is in it really can make a difference. It's a room to unwind and relax, so we can get on with changing things around, so you feel a change in the air as soon as you enter the room.

First, I must stress the need for you to get those electronic devices out of your bedroom. By all accounts, the bedroom should be a place to rest and not to lie in bed watching a movie on television or checking out the Internet via your laptop.

The Bed.

You should attempt to make your bed as luxurious and sumptuous as you possibly can. This means a quality duvet, thick pillows, and throws that just make you want to snuggle down and effectively hibernate. Also, try to invest in a quality mattress as you should attempt to have the best quality nights sleep that you possibly can.

Oh, and if possible, position your bed, so you have the best view possible out of your window in the morning; that's if you have a view worth talking about.

The Floor.

If you have carpet, then replace it when it gets a bit worn down as you should be looking for something that is thick and basically tickles the soles of your feet as you walk on it. If you have wooden floors, then I would recommend that you get a statement rug. This should also be thick and luxurious and just feel amazing when you are standing on it. The rug should also be quite large, so it is not lost in the room.

The Lights.

Soft lights are the order of the day, and how about going for some kind of vintage or antique style light to add a touch of class? You should have one on either side of the bed and if possible get lamps that have different settings to alter how bright they are so you can change things as the mood takes you.

Decor.

The bedroom can be a place where you really push the boundaries a bit with the color scheme. For example, you might want to make the walls a dark gray if you have a lot of natural light coming in, but if the light is limited, then scrap that idea. When that is mixed with light bedding, then you have a good balance in your bedroom.

Adding that Final Touch of Hygge.

I've mentioned the bedding, but if you have a lot of light coming into the room, then this can also be a good place for you to have that quiet spot and just read or let your mind drift away to more pleasant things. A chair in the corner is perfect especially if you have a nice view out of the bedroom window.

Organization is massive with hygge, so having your wardrobe perfect is going to really be essential. You need to think about coordinating things and understanding where everything is in an instant. Getting stressed out when you are trying to get ready is far from ideal, but then dressing is something that is a completely different topic.

Consider having your bedroom as a place where you can pamper yourself, and for any females reading this who get themselves ready in their bedroom, then use organizers and make a real thing out of it with a dressing table. Have quality mirrors, keep the place spotless, and have lavender scented sachets in drawers to keep things smelling amazing. A nice linen spray will also work wonders.

By doing a number of small things, your bedroom can become a haven just like you have always wanted it to be. We are not talking about wholesale changes, just comfortable additions to the room that will lead to an amazing sleep.

Hygge and the Conservatory

I'm adding this section in with its own chapter even though there may be a number of readers that will look at it and wonder what on earth I'm talking about. Well, that is absolutely fine, but for those that do have this form of extension, then read on.

Of course, with a conservatory, you are hardly going to be short of light flooding in thanks to it mainly being made up of huge glass windows. That fits in perfectly with what hygge is trying to get you to achieve.

In this instance, my main focus would be on that link between the home and nature outside. The fact it is surrounded by glass allows you to include a number of plants just to add some life. However, don't go crazy and turn it into a jungle as they should be more akin to splashes of life rather than a conservatory that is part greenhouse.

Also, I would go with a very comfortable suite to lounge around on and natural blinds to give you some privacy in the evening. This should be accompanied with candles in various parts and if you are in a colder part of the world, then some heating is essential just to keep it all comfortable.

Oh, I would also make sure that the garden you are looking out on is attractive even in the evening as it provides a better backdrop for your conservatory. Keep toys out of there if you have children and do not bring any electronics into this space. A conservatory is supposed to be relaxing so keep it that way.

Bringing it All Together

My hope is that through this book you have been able to get a clear idea of what hygge is all about and how to then go ahead and implement it into your own home. I'm not saying that you have to follow these steps word for word. They are merely ideas to effectively get the ball rolling in your mind and perhaps even inspire you onto other things.

Now, I do accept that I've covered a whole host of things, and it can be tough to try to really get to grips with what you should do next. Keeping that thought firmly at the front of your mind, I'd recommend you doing the following.

- Take your time in assessing your home room by room.

- Do it one step at a time.

- Focus on clutter at first to free up space.

- Next, make full use of the light that comes into your home.

- Look at understanding the purpose of each part of a room.

- Be methodical in your approach.

- Don't forget the outside of your home as well.

- For colors, keep with tonal colors rather than having too many.

- Use candles and small lamps to create an atmosphere.

- Don't forget the scents. They help immensely.

- Music should be played, but in the background, so you can still chat.

- Take pride in the smaller things in your home that bring the most joy.

There are actually so many different things to mention, but then perhaps the final thing that I would like to say about hygge is that it all comes down to you doing things in your home that bring you pleasure. If it makes you feel content about being there, then who am I to tell you that this is wrong?

Yes, the Danes like to keep things white, use a mixture of materials, and have the best storage in existence, but it doesn't overall mean that you need to follow suit. Understand what is comfortable to you and what will make you feel excited about being home, and stick with that. Your home is personal to you and only you know what works best of all so just take the things I've discussed throughout this book as a rough guideline for you to work from.

Now, go out there and get on with it. Turn your home into the coziest and most comfortable home that you have ever known.

Win a free

kindle
OASIS

Let us know what you thought of this book to enter the
sweepstake at:

http://booksfor.review/hyggehome

Printed in Great Britain
by Amazon